DINOSAUR WORLDS

RISE OF THE
DINOSAURS

DON LESSEM

Heinemann

DINOSAUR WORLDS: RISE OF THE DINOSAURS
was produced by Bender Richardson White,Uxbridge, UK.

Editors: Lionel Bender, Andy Boyles
Designer: Ben White
Editorial Assistants: John Stidworthy, Madeleine Samuel
Media Conversion and Typesetting:
  Peter MacDonald and Diacritic
Production: Kim Richardson
Senior Scientific Consultant: Dr Peter Dodson, Professor of
Anatomy and Geology at the University of Pennsylvania
School of Veterinary Medicine, and Vice-President of the
Dinosaur Society.

First published in the USA in 1996 by
Highlights for Children, Honesdale, Pennsylvania 18431.

This edition published in Great Britain in 1996 by
Heinemann Children's Reference, an imprint
of Heinemann Educational Publishers, a division of Reed
Educational and Professional Publishing Limited,
Halley Court, Jordan Hill, Oxford OX2 8EJ.

MADRID ATHENS
FLORENCE PRAGUE WARSAW
PORTSMOUTH NH CHICAGO SAO PAULO MEXICO
SINGAPORE TOKYO MELBOURNE AUCKLAND
IBADAN GABORONE JOHANNESBURG KAMPALA NAIROBI

© 1996 Highlights for Children, USA

ISBN 0 431 05658 7 Hb   ISBN 0 431 05663 3 Pb

British Library Cataloguing-in-Publication Data.
A catalogue record for this book is available
from the British Library.

Printed in Spain

**This book is recommended by the Dinosaur Society UK.
For more information please contact The Dinosaur Society UK,
P O Box 329, Canterbury, Kent, CT4 5GB**

Acknowledgements
Photographs Pages: 5: Dr Paul Sereno/Matrix Photo Agency.
10: Don Lessem. 14–15: Bruce Coleman Collection. 16: Dr Paul
Sereno. 20 and 27: Dr Martin Sander, Bonn University. 24–25:
Norbert Rosing/Oxford Scientific Films. 31: Don Lessem. 34–35:
James H. Robinson/Oxford Scientific Films. 36 (left), 37 (right):
Paul E. Olsen, Lamont-Doherty Earth Observatory of Columbia
University. 36–37: Breck P. Kent/Oxford Scientific Films.
40: Dr Mike Raath, Port Elizabeth Museum, South Africa.
44: George W. Frame. 47 (top left, top right): Dr Anusuya
Chinsamy-Turan, South African Museum, Cape Town.
47 (bottom): Dr Mike Raath.
Illustrations All double-page scenes by Steve Kirk. All other major
illustrations by James Field. Ecology diagrams and small featured
creatures by Jim Robins. Step-by-step sequences by John James.
Maps by Ron Hayward. Cover illustration by Steve Kirk.

GLOSSARY

The Triassic Period lasted from 245 million to 208 million years ago. In the Late Triassic Period, dinosaurs were often not the most common vertebrates. Other less familiar animals included:

Aetosaurs (ay-EE-toe-saws) Plant-eating reptiles that resembled crocodiles with stubby snouts.
Cynodonts (SY-no-donts) Mammal-like reptiles with dog-like teeth.
Dicynodonts (die-SY-no-donts) Mammal-like plant-eating reptiles.
Ichthyosaurs (ICK-thee-o-saws) Fish-shaped air-breathing marine reptiles.
Labyrinthodonts (LAB-uh-RIN-tho-donts) Fat-bodied amphibians of many forms and sizes, most of which had a pattern like a maze (or labyrinth) inside their teeth.
Phytosaurs (FY-toe-saws) Armoured crocodile-like reptiles that lived mostly in water, but also on land.
Protosuchians (PRO-toe-SOO-key-uns) Early long-legged land crocodiles
Pterosaurs (TAIR-o-SAWS) Flying reptiles, the first backboned animals to fly. Among them were Pterodactyls (TAIR-o-DACK-tills) and Rhamphorhynchids (RAM-fo-RING-kids).
Rauisuchians (RAO-ih-SOO-key-uns) Meat-eating reptiles of the Triassic Period.
Rhynchosaurs (RINK-o-saws) Pig-sized plant-eaters with beaks like parrots, common in the Late Triassic.
Sphenodontids (SFEE-no-DON-tids) Small lizard-like reptiles of the Late Triassic. One kind – the tuatara of New Zealand – still lives.
Sphenosuchians (SFEE-no-SOO-key-uns) Small, long-legged land reptiles that were among the earliest crocodiles.
Thecodonts (THEE-ko-donts) Mostly meat-eaters, these were the earliest of the 'ruling reptiles'. They included ancestors of dinosaurs, aetosaurs, phytosaurs and rauisuchians.
Therapsids (ther-AP-sids) Mammal-like reptiles of two groups: dicynodonts and the cynodonts.

ECOLOGICAL TERMS

carnivore a meat-eating animal.
climate the average weather conditions in a particular part of the world.
environment the total living conditions, including landscape, climate, plants and animals.
evolved changed, over many generations, to produce a new species, body feature or way of life.
geography the study of the land, sea and air on Earth.
geology the study of the makeup of Earth and its rocks, minerals and fossils.
habitat the area in which an animal or plant lives, for example, a desert, forest or lake.
herbivore a plant-eating animal.
migrate to move from place to place as conditions change.
predator a carnivore that hunts and kills.
prey an animal that is hunted and eaten by a predator; also, the act of hunting, catching and eating an animal.
scavenger a carnivore that does not kill its prey but eats the bodies of animals already dead.
species a group of living things in which individuals look alike and can reproduce with one another.
vegetation plant life.

ABOUT THIS BOOK

Welcome to *Dinosaur Worlds*. In these pages you will see dinosaurs as you have never seen them before – with their fellow animals and plants in the environments they inhabited. Dinosaurs were a highly successful and varied group of land reptiles with fully upright postures and S-curved necks that lived from 228 million to 65 million years ago.

Rise of the Dinosaurs explores the environments of the first dinosaurs, from 230 to 200 million years ago, and traces their success in a time of great changes. This book reveals their worlds as today's leading scientists and artists see them, based on fossil records. Fossils are the remains of once-living creatures that have been preserved in the rocks. Comparisons with living animals and habitats help to fill in details that fossils cannot provide.

This book is divided into four main chapters, each looking at a specific dinosaur fossil site and revealing a different feature of dinosaur life and death. A short introductory section provides background information about the world at that time. It also contains a visual explanation of scientific and technical terms used in the book.

Enjoy your journey of discovery to the lost worlds of the dinosaurs!

"Dino" Don Lessem

Measurements
This book uses metric units of measure:
      centimetre (cm) , metre (m),
      kilogram (kilo) and tonne
1 cm = 0.4 inch, 1m = 40 inches = 3.3 feet
1 kilo = 2.2 pounds
1 tonne (1,000 kilos) is approximately 1 ton

CONTENTS

Within each chapter of the book are five double-page spreads. The first spread is a large dramatic scene at the site millions of years ago. The second spread, 'A Look Back In Time', identifies and describes the major animals and plants in the scene and highlights the environment. The next spread, 'Featured Creatures', gives basic facts and figures about the most interesting animals and plants. Spread four, 'Then And Now', compares dinosaurs and their worlds with present-day animals and habitats. The last spread in each chapter, 'How Do We Know?', looks at the scientific evidence for all this – the fossils found at the site and what they reveal about the behaviour and ecology of dinosaurs.

LATE TRIASSIC PERIOD

CLIMATE

The first dinosaurs evolved from reptiles in the Late Triassic Period, nearly 230 million years ago. They were one of many new groups of land creatures, just as other new life forms were conquering the air and the sea. All of the Earth's slowly shifting land was joined into one supercontinent along the equator, and the climate everywhere was warm and growing drier. Conifer trees, palm-like cycads and ferns grew wherever there was enough water. Grass, flowering plants and the broad-leaved trees we know today had not yet evolved.

FOSSIL FINDS AROUND THE WORLD

This map shows the present-day continents and the dinosaur fossil sites from the Late Triassic and Early Jurassic Periods. The four sites featured in this book are shown in red. **The Valley of the Moon** in northwestern Argentina was home to the first dinosaurs we know well.

Western Europe was one of the first areas to be inhabited by plant-eating dinosaurs, the prosauropods. Fossils found in **Nova Scotia** reveal the time when large reptiles died out while plant- and meat-eating dinosaurs prospered.

The climate of the Late Triassic grew drier as the period drew to a close, 208 million years ago, especially in the centre of the continent. Occasionally, heavy rains swept across the land, swelling lakes and rivers. Around these wetter areas, plant and animal life was especially rich.

CONTINENTS
Around 230 million years ago, there was just one land mass now called Pangaea. This supercontinent straddled the equator. By the end of the Triassic Period, Pangaea had begun to split apart. Within the following Jurassic Period, two giant land masses, Gondwana in the south and Laurasia in the north, would form.

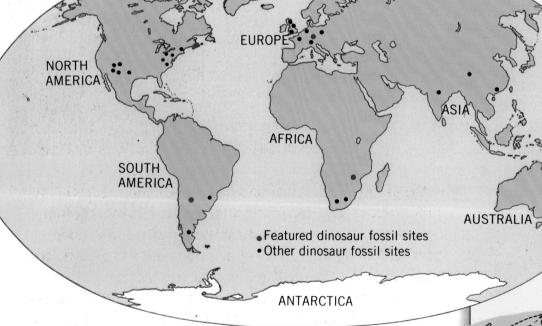

Featured dinosaur fossil sites
Other dinosaur fossil sites

Below
Green areas: the continents in Triassic times. Black outlines: original position of the modern continents.

Fossils from **southern Africa** have given scientists some of the best evidence of how dinosaurs grew. Triassic fossils have been found in many places around the world. But these sites were closer together then. As Pangaea broke up, they were scattered across the globe.

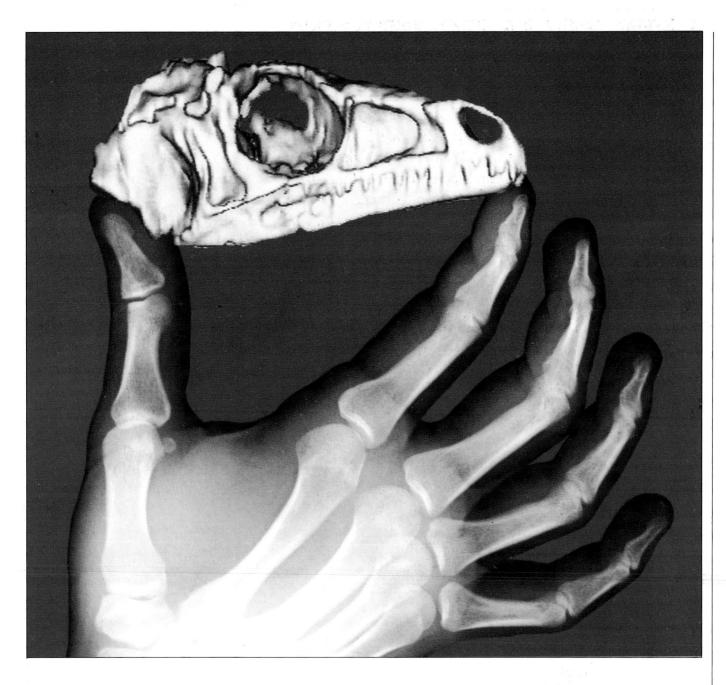

Fossil find

The tiny skull of the meat-eating dinosaur *Eoraptor* (see page 12) is held between the thumb and forefinger of palaeontologist Dr Paul Sereno – in an X-ray photograph. Dr Sereno found and named the fossil in 1993. The large hole at the centre was filled by the eyeballs, and the hole at the tip of the snout was the location of the nostrils. At the rear of the skull was the braincase.

In the Late Triassic, mammals had not yet appeared, and their mouse-like reptile ancestors were dwarfed by giant reptiles. These big animals included fat-bodied, plant-eating land reptiles. Among them, the pig-like rhynchosaurs and the cow-sized dicynodonts were the most widespread.

Towards the end of the Triassic Period and the beginning of the Jurassic Period big plant-eaters, the prosauropod dinosaurs, emerged. The meat-eaters on land included both the solidly built, straight-legged phytosaurs and the first meat-eating dinosaurs. Unlike most reptiles, Late Triassic and Early Jurassic carnivorous dinosaurs were swift. They ran on two legs positioned directly beneath their bodies.

A TRIASSIC DINOSAUR: *Plateosaurus*

Scientists and artists try to reconstruct prehistoric life and to understand how these plants and animals might have lived. To bring the past to life in our imaginations, they need more than fossils.

Bones do not hold the answer to every question about an animal's behaviour, size, age, diet, skin or internal organs. But scientists can make reasonable guesses about these details by comparing extinct creatures with living animals. They assume that ancient animals, like dinosaurs, had many bodily features and functions similar to those of modern animals. In addition, some basic ideas about ecology – such as the energy and food chain – seem to hold true for many different kinds of environments. Here we show how some of this knowledge is applied to prehistoric life.

GEOLOGICAL TIME

Dinosaurs lived during the Mesozoic Era, or 'Middle time of life on Earth', which is divided into three periods: the Triassic, Jurassic and Cretaceous. Scientists divide the Triassic Period (245 to 208 million years ago) into three parts: Early, Middle and Late. Dinosaurs appeared during the Late Triassic, 228 million years ago.

ENERGY AND FOOD CHAIN

Living things need energy to live and grow. Sunlight contains energy. Plants trap, or 'fix', this energy to make their food from water and carbon dioxide gas. When animals eat plants, they capture some of this energy. Meat-eaters get their energy by feeding on plant-eaters. Decomposers and scavengers – at the end of the 'food chain' – get their energy from dead animals and plants. Some dinosaurs got their energy from plants, some by eating other animals.

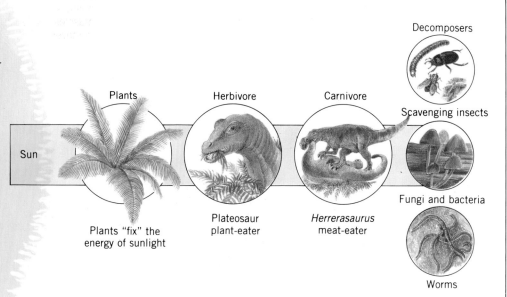

Sun

Plants

Plants "fix" the energy of sunlight

Herbivore

Plateosaur plant-eater

Carnivore

Herrerasaurus meat-eater

Decomposers

Scavenging insects

Fungi and bacteria

Worms

BONY TENDONS

Tendons like those that allowed *Plateosaurus* to hold its tail stiffly off the ground sometimes become fossils. Fleshy tendons do not fossilize.

DINOSAUR SKIN

This had scales and small bumps called tubercles. There are fossil impressions of dinosaur skin but we have no idea how dinosaur skin was coloured.

This cutaway drawing of a *Plateosaurus*, a plant-eater, shows the major parts of a dinosaur. Soft tissues, such as muscles and guts, rarely become fossilized because these parts decompose quickly. Dinosaur fossils are most often found in dry areas that were moist lowlands when the dinosaur died. Bones, eggs, dung, footprints and skin can become fossils.

BONES
Bones are joined together as a skeleton, allowing body movement.

JAWS
An animal's jaws are equipped with teeth needed to break up food material. *Plateosaurus* had many small teeth for shredding plants.

THE SKULL
This protects the brain and houses the main sense organs: the eyes, ears, nose and tongue. Prosauropods, such as *Plateosaurus*, had small brains for their body size, so they probably were not especially intelligent animals.

THE BACKBONE
Also known as the spine, this is made up of bones called vertebrae. An animal with a backbone is called a vertebrate.

THE RIB CAGE
This protects the heart and lungs.

THE SKELETON
This is a rigid framework that supports an animal's body, protects its internal parts and provides attachment points for muscles involved in movement.

THE GUTS
The guts process food. They consist of the stomach and intestines. Prosauropods must have had large stomachs and long intestines to digest all the plants they consumed.

BLOOD
Blood flows through the body in vessels, which are like thin pipes or tubes. It carries heat, food and oxygen to all parts of the body and takes away waste material. **Warm-blooded animals** can keep a steady body temperature despite changes in the environment. **Cold-blooded animals** have a body temperature that changes with the environment. They warm themselves by basking in sunlight and cool down by moving into shade or water. *Plateosaurus* was probably cold-blooded.

MUSCULAR ORGANS
Organs such as the heart and stomach, work like pumps. Skeletal muscles pull bones to produce movement.

HANDS
A dinosaur used its hands not only for grasping and tearing, but also to fight off enemies.

POSTURE, OR STANCE
This is the way an animal stands. Vertebrates like ourselves stand on the hind legs and have an upright posture. Other vertebrates stand on all four legs. Unlike most reptiles, dinosaurs walked on their toes, with their legs directly beneath their bodies. *Plateosaurus* walked mainly on all fours but also moved around on only its sturdy hind legs.

PELVIS, OR HIPS
The hipbone, which links the backbone to the hind limbs, is not a single bone but a combination of three pairs of bones. Each side consists of an ilium, an ischium and a pubis. Differences in the pubis mark the two major types of dinosaurs. **Lizard-hipped dinosaurs** have a pubis that points forwards and down. In **bird-hipped dinosaurs**, the pubis points backwards and down, alongside the ischium. *Plateosaurus* was lizard-hipped.

FOSSILS
Fossils are parts or traces of once-living things that are preserved in rocks. Bones fossilize most often when sediment – sand and mud from rivers – covers the bone. Then minerals enter the bone, preserving it.

DAWN OF THE DINOSAURS
VALLEY OF THE MOON
Northwestern Argentina

228 million years ago

Beside a riverbank, huge plant-eaters browse on ferns, and a pig-sized herbivore has been killed by a new form of killer, a meat-eating dinosaur. This dinosaur, in turn, is preyed upon by a big reptilian hunter and by a smaller dinosaur.

NORTHWESTERN ARGENTINA

The first dinosaurs appeared about 230 million years ago, when the world's land was one giant continent. In what is now a desert in northwestern Argentina, the warm, lush riverbanks were home to many creatures. Here, scientists have discovered many spectacular skeletons of early dinosaurs and other even larger reptiles.

Soaring over the riverbanks were the first flying reptiles, the pterosaurs. In the water and on the land, crocodile-like creatures prowled. Some were as small as domestic cats. Others were as large as small lorries. Several of these animals had flat teeth, specialized for chewing plants. Others had sharper teeth for killing other animals.

The largest animals in this world were not dinosaurs but rauisuchians – meat-eating reptiles like *Saurosuchus*. Other large animals around at this time were the slow-moving plant-eaters, the dicynodonts. They had strong muscles in the back of their skulls. Their jaws could slide back and forth to slice plants. The most common animals of all in Late Triassic Argentina were the rhynchosaurs. These were plant-eaters the size of pigs, with beaks like those of parrots.

A spider builds a web among the branches to trap its insect prey. Other small creatures, such as therapsids (see page 13) and lizards, also ate insects.

Valley of the Moon – Today The riverbanks where dinosaurs first roamed dried up millions of years ago. Today's 'badlands' - an upland dry area with deep gullies formed by flash floods - look like the surface of the Moon, giving the valley its popular name.

A small meat-eating dinosaur called an *Eoraptor* peeks around the base of a conifer tree. With its keen eyesight, speed and grasping hands, *Eoraptor* is an efficient hunter of small creatures and larger, slower plant-eaters. This *Eoraptor* has seen a tiny mouse-like therapsid that is feeding among fungi and ferns. Even in a slight breeze, the leaves of these delicate plants rustle. The therapsid hears the hunter and might escape.

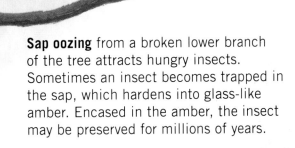

Sap oozing from a broken lower branch of the tree attracts hungry insects. Sometimes an insect becomes trapped in the sap, which hardens into glass-like amber. Encased in the amber, the insect may be preserved for millions of years.

Valley of the Moon – Then
Along the riverbanks, ferns and araucarian conifer trees grew lush and tall. Meat-eaters included crocodile-like *Saurosuchus* and a wolf-sized cynodont called *Exaeretodon*. *Eoraptor*, a dog-sized dinosaur, might have both hunted and scavenged. *Herrerasaurus* was a larger predatory dinosaur. *Scaphonyx* was a large rhynchosaur with many rows of teeth and a parrot-like beak for nipping plants. Dicynodonts had powerful jaws and two tusks that could cut tough plant fibres. Sphenosuchians may have clambered into the trees in search of food.

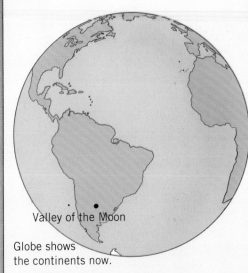

Valley of the Moon

Globe shows the continents now.

Argentina, Then and Now Today, Argentina is 2,300 kilometres south of the equator. It is cooler and drier now than it was in the Late Triassic, when it sat on the equator.

THE DINOSAURS EMERGE

The Valley of the Moon was home to some of the first dinosaurs we know about. They stood upright and were fast-moving killers. The overall design of meat-eating dinosaurs, as two-legged runners with powerful jaws as weapons, helped them to be successful until the end of the dinosaurs' reign.

Eoraptor and *Herrerasaurus* were among the earliest dinosaurs known. *Eoraptor* is a recently discovered dinosaur, and fossils of both have been excavated from rocks of similar age in the Valley of the Moon. Like modern reptiles, these creatures probably had scaly skin and laid eggs. They were small compared to some later meat-eating dinosaurs. But among the animals of their time, they showed several new features special to dinosaurs. For example, they walked on their toes, with their legs positioned directly beneath them and their tails held off the ground.

HERRERASAURUS

Meaning of name: 'Herrera's lizard', named after Victorino Herrera who discovered it
Order: Saurischia
Size, Weight: 3 to 6 metres long, 360 to 450 kilos
Locations: Northwestern Argentina, possibly southwestern United States
Diet: Meat

With its large jaws, *Herrerasaurus* might have swallowed small animals whole, as a present-day snake does. But more often it probably used its strong jaws and sharp teeth to gnaw and bite its prey.

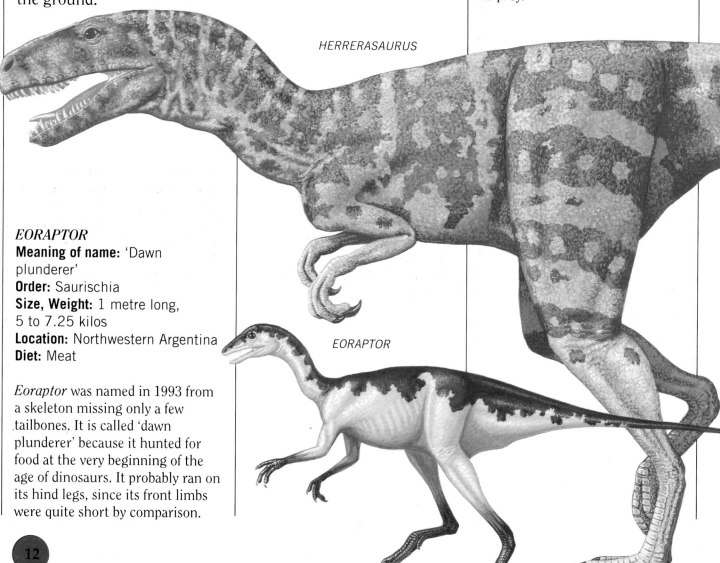

HERRERASAURUS

EORAPTOR

EORAPTOR

Meaning of name: 'Dawn plunderer'
Order: Saurischia
Size, Weight: 1 metre long, 5 to 7.25 kilos
Location: Northwestern Argentina
Diet: Meat

Eoraptor was named in 1993 from a skeleton missing only a few tailbones. It is called 'dawn plunderer' because it hunted for food at the very beginning of the age of dinosaurs. It probably ran on its hind legs, since its front limbs were quite short by comparison.

INSECTS

In the boggy conditions around streams and ponds, many kinds of insects flew through the air. They included grasshopper-like creatures with wings 30 cm long. Lizards and amphibians preyed on the insects.

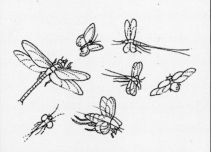

Standing up

Why did the dinosaurs survive and flourish when most other big animals of the Late Triassic died 208 million years ago? The first dinosaurs were probably no more intelligent than other large animals of their time. But dinosaurs were faster because they ran on two legs beneath their bodies. So perhaps they were better hunters than others in the Late Triassic.

The therapsids were ancestors of the first mammals, which appeared soon after this time. Early mammals remained small animals, no bigger than pet cats, while dinosaurs were alive.

Dinosaur with upright posture

Megazostrodon – an early type of mammal

PLANTS

A dense forest of evergreen trees called araucarians covered the valley of the first dinosaurs. In the shade of these odd umbrella-shaped trees, hardy ferns and other non-flowering plants grew. The treetops spread out like fans more than 30 metres above the ground.

SAUROSUCHUS

SAUROSUCHUS
Meaning of name: 'Lizard crocodile'
Order: Rauisuchia
Size, Weight: 6 metres long, 1,000 kilos
Location: Northwestern Argentina
Diet: Meat

Saurosuchus was the largest rauisuchian. It may have resembled a crocodile, but it lived on land. *Saurosuchus* walked with its legs positioned further under the body than do modern lizards, but it did not walk or run as efficiently as dinosaurs did.

FOOTHILL FORESTS

No place in the world today is exactly like northwestern Argentina 228 million years ago. And there exist no life forms resembling the creatures that lived then in the region. But the forests at the base of the Rocky Mountains in western Wyoming in the United States have some important features in common with the environment of the ancient Valley of the Moon.

As in Triassic Argentina, these forests are mainly made up of tall conifers, with few plants in the deep shade of the trees. Large and small predators, such as wolves, badgers and weasels, live here and feed on a variety of large plant-eaters, including deer, elk and moose. Because modern and prehistoric carnivores faced the same basic problem of hunting and killing large animals for food, it is possible that they had similar ways of solving these problems. For example, predatory dinosaurs might have hunted in packs, as wolves do. Does that mean that they also had sophisticated ways of communicating with one another? Is it possible that they might have lived together in groups?

Though no bigger than a small dog, *Eoraptor* may have been much more vicious. Perhaps it hunted in packs, using its speed to ambush prey like this young dicynodont.

In most places, including ancient Argentina and modern Wyoming, large meat-eaters prey on plant-eaters and small meat-eaters. Some hunting dinosaurs in the Valley of the Moon may have stalked prey on their own, as the bobcat does today in Wyoming. And like the bobcat, they may have hunted within separate areas of the forest so as not to compete with one another for any available prey.

In the snow, a bobcat kitten stands over its prey – a snowshoe hare. *Eoraptor* possibly hunted and killed like the bobcat, catching its victims with its claws, then using its sharp teeth to tear at the meat. In western North America, bobcats, coyotes, pumas and wolves are all hunters of plant-eaters. And like the carnivorous dinosaurs, they can outrun or outwit their prey.

Scientists think that in ancient Argentina the biggest predator, *Saurosuchus* **(1)**, ate lumbering plant-eaters like dicynodonts **(2)**. *Herrerasaurus* **(3)** fed on smaller, crocodile-like animals **(4)**, and *Eoraptor* **(5)** ate small prey. There was more food for plant-eaters, and their meals were easier to obtain, so they easily outnumbered the meat-eaters.

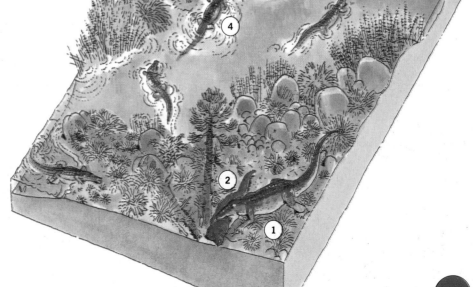

DAWN OF THE DINOSAURS

For many years, the Valley of the Moon has been known to scientists as the richest source of fossils from the time of the earliest dinosaurs. Remains of *Herrerasaurus*, a predatory dinosaur (see page 12), were first discovered there in the 1950s. But *Herrerasaurus* and many other creatures from this remote desert became well known only in recent years, after scientists examined the fossils in detail in the laboratory.

No fossil tells as much about the appearance and origins of an animal as its skull. Several bones of *Herrerasaurus* (but no skull) were discovered years ago. In 1988, American palaeontologist Dr Paul Sereno found the first skull of *Herrerasaurus* while he was walking alone in the desert. It was so well preserved that even the bony rings in its eye sockets were still there.

A tiny bone in *Herrerasaurus*'s ears indicates that this dinosaur may have had a keen sense of hearing. Its long claws and sharp-toothed jaws suggest it was a fearsome hunter and killer. *Herrerasaurus*'s upright posture suggests that it was agile and swift for its day.

Remains of a *Herrerasaurus*
The fossilized skull, neck and forelimb of a *Herrerasaurus* lie in rock in the Valley of the Moon. Next to the fossils, a palaeontologist's brush, used for clearing away loose dirt, gives an indication of the size of the bones.

LOST AND FOUND

An aging *Herrerasaurus* breathes its last on the bank of a shallow lake in the Valley of the Moon. All around it, life goes on. But this *Herrerasaurus*, unlike most others, will become a fossil, as shown in this sequence of illustrations.
   In shallow water, the dinosaur's carcass bloats with gases produced by microbes as its flesh rots **(1)**. Insects, bacteria and other decomposers eat *Herrerasaurus*'s flesh **(2)**. Within weeks of the dinosaur's death, its soft parts are gone. Just the bones and teeth will be left. These become buried in sand **(3)**.

Minerals from the lake bed enter holes where blood vessels and nerves once ran through *Herrerasaurus*'s bones. The bones fossilize.

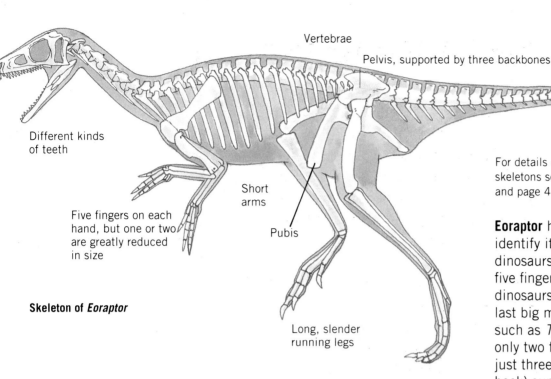

Vertebrae

Pelvis, supported by three backbones

Different kinds
of teeth

Five fingers on each
hand, but one or two
are greatly reduced
in size

Short
arms

Pubis

Skeleton of *Eoraptor*

Long, slender
running legs

For details of dinosaur
skeletons see also pages 6-7
and page 45.

Eoraptor had several features that
identify it as one of the first
dinosaurs. For example, it had
five fingers. Later meat-eating
dinosaurs had fewer fingers. The
last big meat-eating dinosaurs,
such as *Tyrannosaurus rex*, had
only two fingers. *Eoraptor* had
just three vertebrae (bones of the
back) supporting its tiny pelvis.
As dinosaurs grew bigger, more
vertebrae supported the pelvis.

Eoraptor also lacked an extra
joint in the middle of its jaw and
did not have an especially large
pubis. These were features of
Herrerasaurus and later meat-
eating dinosaurs.

On a second trip to the Valley of the Moon in 1993, Dr Sereno
and his colleagues uncovered a well-preserved and nearly entire
skeleton of *Eoraptor*. In its skull (see page 5), the back teeth
were grooved like the steak-knife teeth of other meat-eating
dinosaurs. But its front teeth were leaf-shaped like those of
plant-eating dinosaurs. Perhaps *Eoraptor* ate plants and meat.

Water levels rise and layers of iron-
rich sand covers much of the
skeleton, turning the bones dark
in colour. Some smaller bones in
the legs and tail are washed
away. Over millions of years,
layers of sand become packed
down and turn to rock above
the fossilized skeleton (4).

As the Valley of the Moon
became a desert in modern
times, winds blew away the layers
of rock. The skull of the dinosaur,
locked in ironstone, was found in
1988 by Dr Sereno (5).

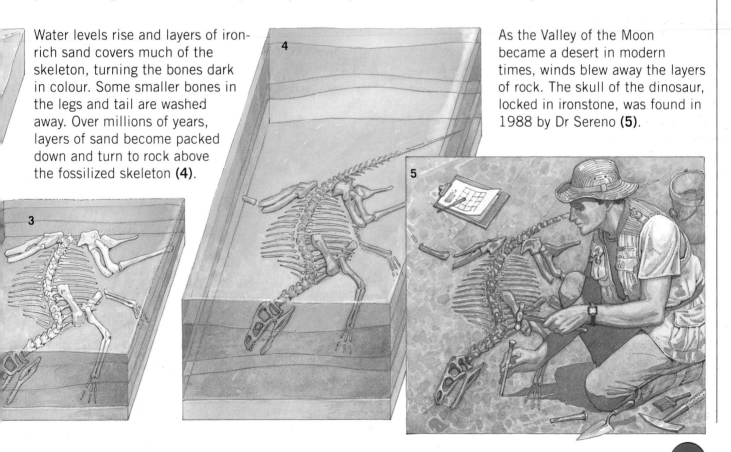

TRAPPED GIANTS
FRICK BRICK
QUARRY
Switzerland
215 million years ago

On the bank of a winding river, a plant-eating *Plateosaurus* plods into the mud in search of food. It soon sinks to its knees, trapped in the muck. Hungry meat-eating dinosaurs close in to feast on the helpless giant.

FEEDING ON PLANTS

Among the ferns and evergreen trees lining the riverbanks 215 million years ago, plant-eating dinosaurs were thriving. Less than 15 million years before, the first dinosaurs – all small meat-eaters – had appeared. By the Late Triassic the plant-eaters were already giants, the biggest animals in their world. Over the next 100 million years, plant-eating dinosaurs would become bigger still.

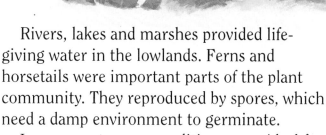

Frick Brick Quarry – Today Many partial fossil skeletons of adult *Plateosaurus* have been found here and at several sites in France and Germany.

The first large plant-eating dinosaurs, such as *Plateosaurus*, could walk on all four legs. They could also stand on just their hind legs to feed. They were the first large animals to exploit the food supply found in the treetops and high branches. Like other plant-eaters, these dinosaurs had big bodies with large stomachs.

Meat-eating dinosaurs also lived along the riverbanks. Crocodile-like reptiles, fish and the first turtles swam in the water. Small flying reptiles soared overhead. In the Late Triassic, the Earth's land was a single continent. The weather was warm and, in most places, dry. In the continent's interior there were desert conditions. At the continent's edges, the effects of the sea made the climate less extreme.

Rivers, lakes and marshes provided life-giving water in the lowlands. Ferns and horsetails were important parts of the plant community. They reproduced by spores, which need a damp environment to germinate.

In some wet areas, conditions were ideal for animals and plants to fossilize after they died and sank into mud. In several parts of the world, fossil beds from this time have been found. Fossils of similar types of animals have been found in China, South America, Greenland and southwestern North America. Scientists think the same kinds of creatures lived worldwide because animals could move around freely on the single world land mass.

Proganochelys, freshwater turtles, search for tadpoles, fish, snails and clams in the water. *Proganochelys* was among the first turtles to develop. Its shell grew to more than 60 cm in length. In addition to a horny beak, *Proganochelys* had teeth in the roof of its mouth. Perhaps these helped hold the slippery fish on which it preyed.

Frick, Switzerland – Then

While one *Plateosaurus* sinks in the mud, in the distance others feed on the fern-like leaves of cycads. Three-metre-long reptiles, *Rutiodon*, members of the phytosaur group, sun themselves on the riverbank.

A *Proganochelys* turtle basks on a mudbank. In the water, a metoposaur, a 2-metre-long amphibian built like a bulky salamander, swims with slow movements of its long tail. Little *Eudimorphodon* pterosaurs, among the earliest of the flying reptiles, fly overhead, looking for fish to seize in jaws that contain 100 teeth. A big meat-eating dinosaur, *Liliensternus*, prowls near the water's edge, watching for unwary prey resting on the riverbank – or stuck in the mud!

GIANTS' ANCESTORS

PLANTS

Calamites, a kind of horsetail, was a common, fast-growing plant along riverbanks. Horsetails grew like reeds, up to 7.5 cm thick and 4.5 metres high. Rings of leaves grew out at intervals up the ribbed stems. At the stem tips were reproductive structures, the cones. Modern horsetails are similar but smaller.

CALAMITES

Large long-necked dinosaurs like *Plateosaurus* may have fed on the tips of *Calamites* or on low-growing ferns and cycads and the lower branches of conifer trees. Smaller plant-eaters could not reach up high enough to get food from the trees. Size and sharp thumb claws appear to have been the plateosaur's only defences against meat-eaters.

Plateosaurs were prosauropod dinosaurs ('pro' meaning before the sauropods). They relied on large gizzards to help them digest plant material that their small jaws were unable to grind well. Their muscular gizzards may have been bigger than footballs. The gizzards may also have contained stomach stones to help break down tough plants. Prosauropods later evolved into sauropods – giant four-legged plant-eaters, the largest of all land animals.

RUTIODON

RUTIODON
Meaning of name: 'Folded tooth' – for the many wrinkles in each of its teeth.
Order: Thecodontia
Size, Weight: 3 to 5 metres long, 230 kilos
Locations: Western Europe, eastern and western North America
Diet: Fish, small reptiles

Rutiodon was a typical phytosaur. It was a heavily armoured crocodile-like meat-eater. *Rutiodon* had a long snout filled with sharp teeth for snatching and eating other reptiles and fish. Phytosaurs were common in the Late Triassic and were lords of the water throughout that period.

PLATEOSAURUS

The anatomy, or body structure, of *Plateosaurus* is illustrated and described in more detail on pages 6 and 7.

PLATEOSAURUS
Meaning of name: 'Broad lizard'
Order: Saurischia
Size, Weight: 6 to 8 metres long, 1 to 2 tonnes
Locations: Western Europe, Greenland
Diet: Plants

Plateosaurus is the best known of all large early plant-eating dinosaurs. The entire skull of *Plateosaurus* was powerfully built. It had many small teeth (see page 7) shaped like leaves with flat sides and serrations, good for shredding plants rather than grinding them.

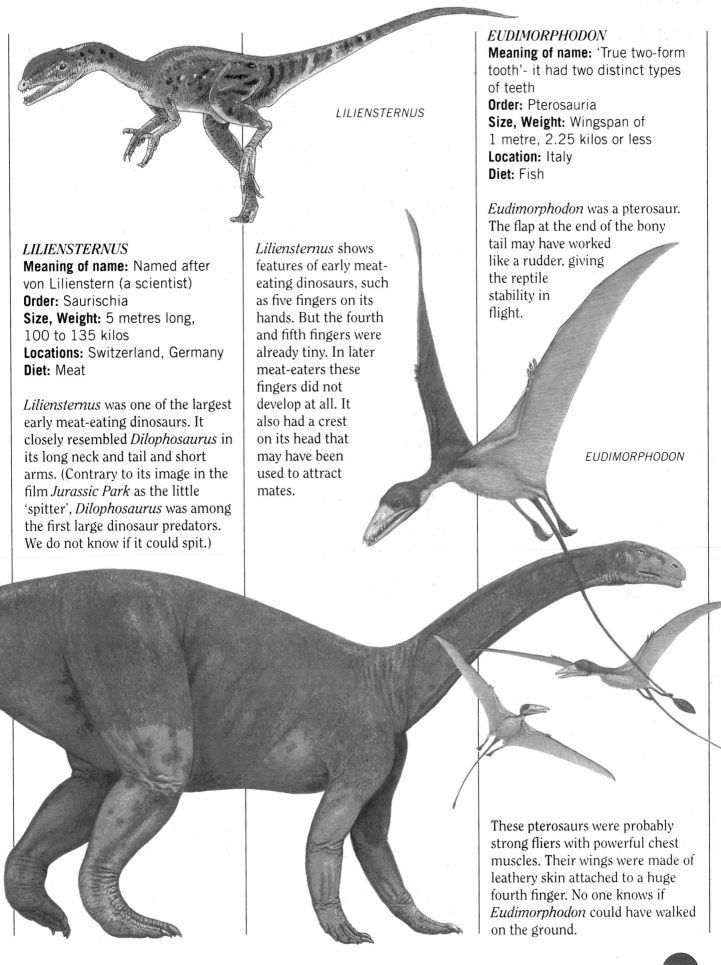

LILIENSTERNUS

EUDIMORPHODON
Meaning of name: 'True two-form tooth'- it had two distinct types of teeth
Order: Pterosauria
Size, Weight: Wingspan of 1 metre, 2.25 kilos or less
Location: Italy
Diet: Fish

Eudimorphodon was a pterosaur. The flap at the end of the bony tail may have worked like a rudder, giving the reptile stability in flight.

LILIENSTERNUS
Meaning of name: Named after von Lilienstern (a scientist)
Order: Saurischia
Size, Weight: 5 metres long, 100 to 135 kilos
Locations: Switzerland, Germany
Diet: Meat

Liliensternus was one of the largest early meat-eating dinosaurs. It closely resembled *Dilophosaurus* in its long neck and tail and short arms. (Contrary to its image in the film *Jurassic Park* as the little 'spitter', *Dilophosaurus* was among the first large dinosaur predators. We do not know if it could spit.)

Liliensternus shows features of early meat-eating dinosaurs, such as five fingers on its hands. But the fourth and fifth fingers were already tiny. In later meat-eaters these fingers did not develop at all. It also had a crest on its head that may have been used to attract mates.

EUDIMORPHODON

These pterosaurs were probably strong fliers with powerful chest muscles. Their wings were made of leathery skin attached to a huge fourth finger. No one knows if *Eudimorphodon* could have walked on the ground.

23

RIVER WORLDS

The environment of the centre of western Europe in the Late Triassic Period was much like that along the River Nile of Egypt today, though the animals and plants differed greatly. Lush vegetation grew along riverbanks that became flooded after heavy rain. Further from the water's edge, the land was generally dry, even desert-like.

The giant reptiles and plant-eating dinosaurs that lived along the riverbanks of Europe 215 million years ago have died out, but some present-day animals in Egypt have lifestyles similar to those of their ancient ancestors.

In the Nile, today's counterparts of the large meat-eating dinosaurs are the crocodiles that patrol the river and its banks in search of prey. Hippopotamuses also live in parts of the River Nile. They come on land to eat large amounts of plants and prefer to feed on the riverbanks. Although adult hippos have no natural predators, their young often fall prey to crocodiles. Fish and reptiles were common then and now. The pterosaurs of the Late Triassic have been replaced by today's wading and fishing birds, such as pelicans.

A cross-section of a riverbank in Switzerland 215 million years ago shows a herd of plateosaurs browsing on the plants beside the river **(1)**. A mud slide caused by heavy rains pours over the vegetation **(2)**. One animal has wandered into the sticky mud and is trapped **(3)**. In this scene, a meat-eating *Liliensternus* **(4)** has seen the plateosaurs and is stalking them. Vegetation is most dense along the banks of the river. It thins out away from the water and gives way to a dry landscape.

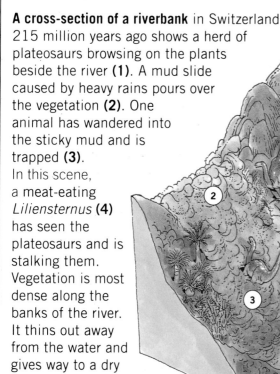

Two ferocious
Liliensternus tear at the throat of a thrashing *Plateosaurus*. Like many modern predators, they may have attacked their prey in the water, which slows the movements of large animals and can prevent them from escaping.

On the banks of the River Nile, a crocodile attacks a young hippo. Crocodiles are related to ancestors of dinosaurs. Today, crocodiles are still fierce predators.

Whether in the modern Nile Valley or in Late Triassic Europe, even large plant-eaters can become victims of meat-eaters, especially when they are injured, trapped or ill. In dry environments like modern Egypt or much of the Late Triassic world, animals gather where food and water are plentiful. When plant-eaters come to feed and drink along the banks of rivers and the shores of lakes, they risk attack from hungry carnivores. A lion, hidden in the grass, waits by a water hole, ready to pounce on any thirsty zebra that comes to drink. In the Late Triassic world, *Liliensternus* probably waited for prey in the same way.

STUCK-IN-THE-MUD DINOSAURS

In quarries across central Europe, dozens of dinosaur skeletons have been found as fossils embedded in Late Triassic rocks. Some of these sites also contain fossils of small plants and small animals. The dinosaur fossils are almost entirely the remains of *Plateosaurus*.

Many plateosaur fossils are preserved with their leg bones intact. The legs are often upright in the rock. This unusual position shows that the dinosaurs were standing when they died and that they stayed in this position after death. Something prevented them from falling. Perhaps they were held in position by stiff mud that later became rock. Scientists think that *Plateosaurus* walked on its back legs, which were longer and stronger than its front limbs. The back legs supported the weight of the animal, which was up to 2 tonnes. The head and forelimbs were balanced by the weight of the tail behind. The heavy stomach was close to the balance point.

Plateosaurus's front limbs might have had several purposes. Each thick forelimb had four fingers and a thumb with a large claw, wide and sharp at its tip. Some scientists think the thumb was used for defence. Others think it helped grab food from trees and bushes. Perhaps this thumb had two functions.

Since plateosaur skeletons are often found in groups, scientists think the animals lived in small herds, as hippos and elephants do today.

Growing bigger and being able to raise their necks allowed prosauropod and sauropod dinosaurs to use new sources of food. The diagram shows:

1. *Plateosaurus* (prosauropod)
2. *Omeisaurus* (sauropod)
3. *Diplodocus* (sauropod)
4. *Brachiosaurus* (sauropod)
5. *Ultrasauros* (sauropod)
6. *Seismosaurus* (sauropod)

Why grow bigger?

Large size is a protection against predators, which prefer to go after the easiest prey to kill. Predators can kill small animals more easily than they can bring down large ones. So small adult animals and the youngsters of large plant-eaters are the main targets. As plant-eating dinosaurs became bigger, they were less likely to be killed by carnivores.

Big animals have to eat large amounts of food to provide the energy their bodies need. But they eat less food for each kilo of their mass than small animals do. Their huge bodies do not lose heat as fast as small animals do. As a result, even low-energy foods like ferns could have provided enough energy for these big dinosaurs to survive.

Without huge energy needs, the giant plant-eaters could travel far on a large stomach full of food. When the plants in one area had been stripped, the herd of giant dinosaurs could trek a great distance to find another food source. Plateosaurs may have travelled long distances between feeding grounds in the way that herding plant-eaters do today.

MASS DEATH

Scientists have discovered more than 140 adult *Plateosaurus* skeletons at a site in Germany. A single story may explain how many of the animals died together.

A herd of plateosaurs **(1)** browses on the muddy bank of a river. The animals edge deeper into the thick sticky mud along the riverbank where the stream recently flooded. The herd is soon knee-deep in ooze **(2)**, with individual plateosaurs thrashing to break free.

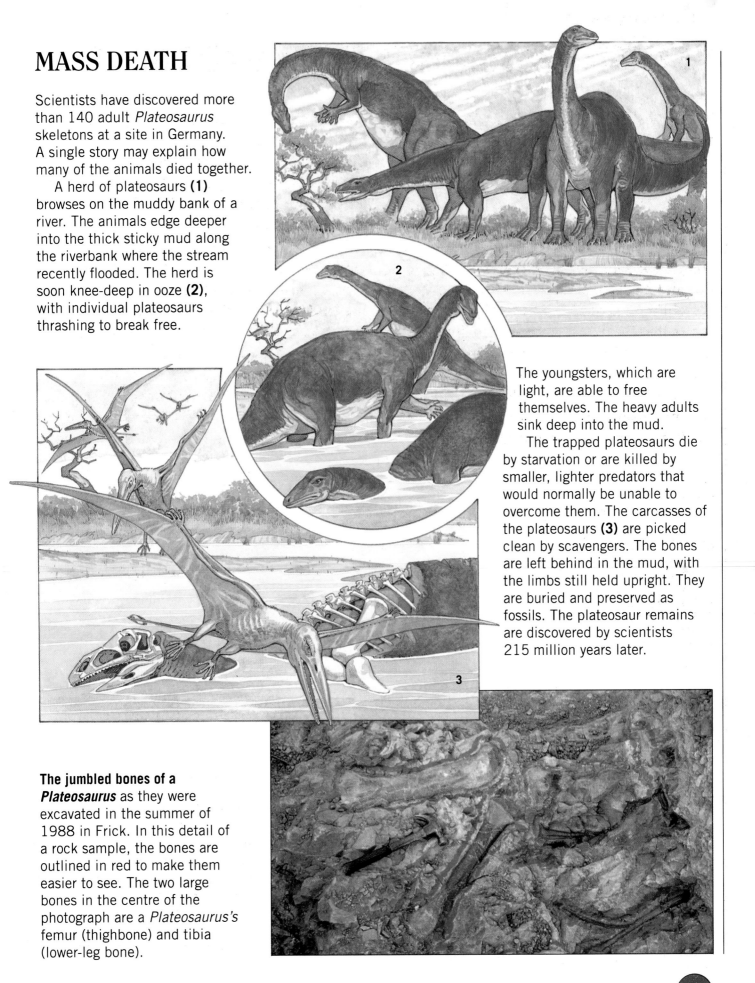

The youngsters, which are light, are able to free themselves. The heavy adults sink deep into the mud.

The trapped plateosaurs die by starvation or are killed by smaller, lighter predators that would normally be unable to overcome them. The carcasses of the plateosaurs **(3)** are picked clean by scavengers. The bones are left behind in the mud, with the limbs still held upright. They are buried and preserved as fossils. The plateosaur remains are discovered by scientists 215 million years later.

The jumbled bones of a *Plateosaurus* as they were excavated in the summer of 1988 in Frick. In this detail of a rock sample, the bones are outlined in red to make them easier to see. The two large bones in the centre of the photograph are a *Plateosaurus's* femur (thighbone) and tibia (lower-leg bone).

EXTINCTION AND SURVIVAL

BAY OF FUNDY
Nova Scotia, Canada
208 million years ago

Panicking reptiles, including small dinosaurs, flee from a forest fire. This disaster is the result of a mysterious worldwide catastrophe that is killing off many species.

DISASTER STRIKES

About 208 million years ago, a mysterious worldwide disaster wiped out many forms of life, ending the Triassic Period and beginning the Jurassic Period. In Nova Scotia and other areas, scientists have found clues about what life was like before and after this mass extinction.

What caused this mass extinction? Scientists have offered several possible explanations. A giant asteroid might have struck the Earth, or changes within the Earth might have triggered a series of volcanic eruptions. Either of these events would have produced drastic changes in the weather. Another possibility is that the slow separation of the world's one land mass into smaller continents would have changed local conditions.

Whatever the cause, small dinosaurs, small land crocodilians and mammal-like reptiles survived the change, while many larger reptiles died out. The plant life changed, too. Bushes and trees with thick evergreen leaves became the most common types.

Small theropods – meat-eating dinosaurs the size of a small child – feed on procolophonids, fat lizard-like creatures whose closest living relatives may be turtles. The procolophonids died out at the end of the Triassic Period, but dinosaurs lived on.

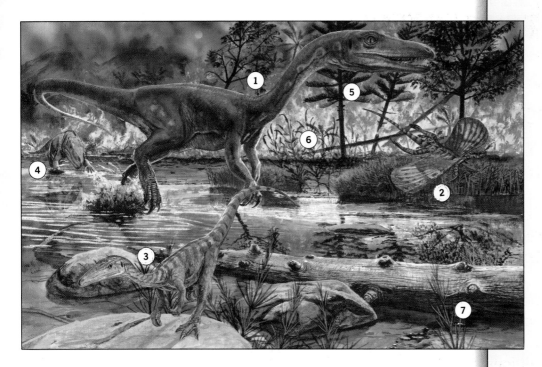

Only a few of the fossils from Late Triassic and Early Jurassic Nova Scotia have been scientifically described and named. Many of the animals of that time look like small versions of familiar creatures known from elsewhere.

ANIMALS
1. *Coelophysis*-like meat-eater (SEE-lo-FY-sis)
2. *Icarosaurus* (ICK-a-ro-SAW-rus)
3. Robin-sized meat-eater
4. Rauisuchian (RAO-y-SOO-key-un)

PLANTS
5. *Classopolis*-like conifer (klass-AW-po-lis)
6. Cycads and ginkgoes
7. Horsetails

Bay of Fundy – Then
Animal and plant life was varied in eastern Canada 208 million years ago, when a great disaster struck the region.

Before the extinction, small meat-eating dinosaurs hunted among such predators as the long-legged rauisuchians. Rauisuchians had also appeared during the Triassic Period, before the dinosaurs. The predatory dinosaurs in Nova Scotia resembled *Coelophysis*, a 3-metre-long carnivore from the American Southwest. Insect-eating reptiles might have included *Icarosaurus*, a lizard that could glide through the air using wings of skin. Ferns, cycads and conifers grew along the shores of shallow lakes.

Bay of Fundy – Today
Palaeontologists hunt for more dinosaur fossils beside the bay, where waves once crashed against the base of tree-topped cliffs.

Nova Scotia, Then and Now
Now Nova Scotia is a province along the rocky northeastern tip of Canada. At the end of the Triassic Period, it was by a shallow sea, not an ocean. It sat on the great dividing line where Pangaea was beginning to split into two continents.

Globe shows the continents now.

Most of the fossils found at the Bay of Fundy are bits and pieces of bone from small animals. Perhaps these creatures survived the disaster because they could hide underground when the climate was harsh. In most extinctions, smaller creatures have survived better than larger ones. At the end of the Permian Period, 245 million years ago, nine out of every ten forms of life were wiped out. Large animals were especially hard-hit.

SMALL WONDERS

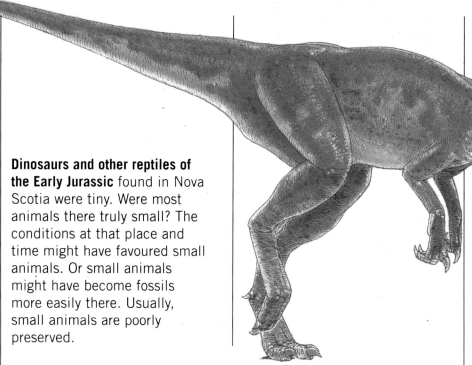

UNNAMED THEROPOD

Dinosaurs and other reptiles of the Early Jurassic found in Nova Scotia were tiny. Were most animals there truly small? The conditions at that place and time might have favoured small animals. Or small animals might have become fossils more easily there. Usually, small animals are poorly preserved.

UNNAMED THEROPOD
Order: Saurischia
Size, Weight: 0.3 to 2.15 metres long, less than 9 kilos
Location: Nova Scotia
Diet: Meat

A small meat-eating dinosaur is known from scattered fossils and footprints in both the Late Triassic and Early Jurassic rocks of Nova Scotia. It appears to have looked like *Coelophysis* (see page 31), a larger meat-eater well known from the American Southwest at this time.

Worldwide, the largest land animals of the Late Triassic Period were crocodile-like reptiles. The mass extinction that ended this period killed these creatures and allowed the dinosaurs to thrive. In Late Triassic Nova Scotia, the giants were rauisuchians and a predator called *Rutiodon* (see pages 13, 22).

Soon after the extinction at the beginning of the Jurassic Period, a variety of dinosaurs lived in Nova Scotia. These dinosaurs included small and large meat-eaters and plant-eaters. Largest of them was a 2.75-metre-long prosauropod, closely related to the dinosaur *Ammosaurus* – known to have grown to 4.25 metres elsewhere in North America.

In the Early Jurassic, another small creature living in Nova Scotia was a two-legged bird-hipped dinosaur (see page 45) that looked like *Lesothosaurus* (see page 43). The plant-eater *Lesothosaurus* lived in southern Africa and grew to a length of about 1 metre. This Nova Scotian relation was no bigger than a turkey. The lizards and crocodilians from Nova Scotia were also small compared to those from other places at this time.

Today, smaller-sized varieties of animals are sometimes found on islands or in places where the environment is difficult to live in. The stresses of everyday life may prevent these animals from reaching their maximum possible size.

Some of the footprints of this as-yet-unnamed theropod were made by an animal no bigger than a robin. The tracks may be those of a youngster. But if they are an adult's, they were made by the smallest dinosaur yet known.

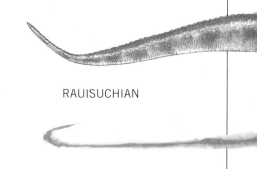

RAUISUCHIAN

ICAROSAURUS

Meaning of name: 'Icarus lizard' (Icarus was a character in Greek mythology that tried to fly using wings of feathers and wax)
Order: Squamata
Size, Weight: 0.5 metre long, 170 grams or less
Locations: Eastern North America, England
Diet: Insects

ICAROSAURUS

RAUISUCHIAN

Meaning of name: 'Rau's crocodile' (Rau is the name of a scientist)
Order: Rauisuchidae
Size, Weight: 6 to 7.5 metres long, 450 kilos or more
Locations: Worldwide
Diet: Meat

This early lizard had very long ribs that could be spread to support a wing of skin used for gliding from branch to branch. The little 'flying dragon' lizards of Southeast Asia glide in the same way today.

The giants of this time were rauisuchians. These were large reptiles with strong hind limbs. Their manner of walking was more efficient than lizards' but not as efficient as dinosaurs'. Rauisuchian fossils are found throughout the Late Triassic world, including along what is now the eastern coast of North America. Scientists think it lived in Nova Scotia as well.

PLANTS

Many kinds of non-flowering plants such as ferns, cycads and evergreen trees lived in Nova Scotia in the Late Triassic Period. But in the Early Jurassic Period of the same area, just a few million years later, most of these plants had disappeared.

Fossil pollen of only one kind of conifer is found here. This conifer, *Classopolis*, grew as both a bush and as a tree. It had very thick needles. Ginkgoes were primitive flowering trees.

CYCADS

Cycads and cycadeoids were common in dinosaur times. These plants bore cones and had thick trunks with flat scales. A fan of leaves spread from their crowns. Cycadeoids are extinct, but cycads are still common in warmer climates today.

TRIASSIC EXTINCTION

After a disaster, life goes on, though many kinds of animals and plants can be wiped out forever. Fast-growing plants, small animals and animals with less specialized needs in diet or habitat are the most likely to survive.

Exploding volcanoes, like the 1982 eruption of Mount St Helens in Oregon in the United States, have both local and worldwide effects. For kilometres around the volcano, fiery lava and thick layers of hot ash kill living things on the ground. High in the atmosphere, gases and ash are blown around the world by winds, causing hazy skies and warmer temperatures.

But not all life is killed around the disaster site. The Mount St Helens eruption did not kill the roots of trees, and new growth soon sprouted from the trunks. Mice and other small burrowing mammals, insects and worms emerged from underground hiding places. More insects, spiders and the seeds of fast-growing plants were blown onto the mountainsides by winds. As insects and plants began to multiply, birds flew in and larger animals returned to the area.

In Nova Scotia at the end of the Triassic Period, a similar pattern of regrowth would have brought back abundant life.

Mount St Helens volcano in Oregon erupted in 1982, with far-reaching damage. The blast was heard over an area of hundreds of square kilometres, and it affected the weather worldwide. Life has already returned to the site.

In the Late Triassic, Nova Scotia was a dry area. Animal and plant life was most abundant along the shores of lakes and rivers. But many shallow lakes were drying up. Dinosaurs and other reptiles, such as the aetosaurs and large phytosaurs shown here, lived in the lush valleys. Reptiles swam in the waters and flew in the skies. Amphibians, fish, insects and mammals lived in this area, too.

At the end of the Triassic Period, many plants and animals became extinct. For the most part, larger animals died. Survivors included many smaller creatures. Their ability to find shelter may have

These fast-growing, spreading herb plants were among the first forms of vegetation to return to the slopes of Mount St Helens following the eruption. This photo was taken about two years after the disaster.

An asteroid, a chunk of rock orbiting the Sun, hurtles to the Earth. Its impact causes changes worldwide, some disastrous for life. Such a disaster is the likely cause of some of the sudden mass extinctions of animals and plants in the Earth's history.

Perhaps the impact of a large asteroid killed off many kinds of animals at the end of the Triassic Period. A cloud of smoke and ash, much the same as a volcanic eruption produces, would have been thrown up into the air. The dust would have blocked the sunlight. This could have led to a drop in temperature worldwide and to the death of those plants that could no longer use the Sun's energy to make food. The effect on plant-eating animals, and on those meat-eaters that fed on them, would have been catastrophic.

helped them survive. Small crocodilians and a variety of fish, little dinosaurs and lizard-like reptiles (as in the scene above), and mammal-like reptiles lived on in Nova Scotia.

In the Early Jurassic Period in Nova Scotia, a new group of plants and animals settled in a very changed land. The environment was moister, yet there were far fewer kinds of plants and animals.

Plant-eating dinosaurs, from small ornithischians to larger prosauropods, were the most abundant animals. Meat-eating dinosaurs, large and small, and crocodilians were also present.

SEARCHING FOR THE REASON

The Bay of Fundy, Nova Scotia, is where fossils best show the drastic change in life across the boundary of the Triassic and Jurassic Periods. From 1988 to 1993, Dr Paul Olsen, Dr Neil Shubin and Dr Hans Sues, three of the world's leading scientific experts on the animals of this time, explored the Bay of Fundy and excavated the fossils.

Their finds and others at the Nova Scotia site include several partial skeletons and thousands of fossil fragments. The fossil animals range in size from reptiles 7.5 metres long to amphibians only a few centimetres in length. Triassic fossils in this part of Canada date from as far back as 225 million years ago. Other fossils found by the bay date from shortly after the start of the Jurassic Period, 208 million years ago.

Close to the changeover in geological periods, the fossil animals and plants show smaller-sized individuals and fewer varieties. This change in fossil types reflects a shift in the environment that must have been drastic and relatively sudden. Footprints and skeletons from Nova Scotia show that in the Jurassic Period, the dinosaurs prospered as plant-eaters and meat-eaters and grew much larger than before.

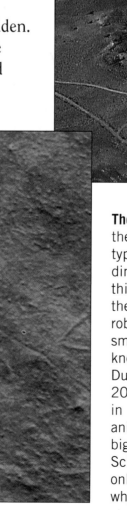

These footprints show the three-toed anatomy typical of meat-eating dinosaurs. The unusual thing about them is that they were made by a robin-sized animal – the smallest dinosaur known (see page 32). During the disaster of 208 million years ago in Nova Scotia, small animals survived and big ones died out. Scientists can make only suggestions about why this should be.

This footprint was left in the Late Triassic mud of the Bay of Fundy by a small, plant-eating dinosaur. The ornithischian, or bird-hipped, dinosaur that made this print was perhaps only 1 metre long – among the smallest of dinosaurs ever found. Footprints and bones found here in rocks from the following Jurassic Period are those of large plant-eating dinosaurs.

'Meteorite Crater' in Arizona is over a kilometre wide and 170 metres deep. It was formed when a fragment of rock from space struck the Earth long after dinosaurs became extinct. Scientists search for much larger craters in the hope of explaining mass extinctions. No such crater has yet been linked to the disaster that ended the Triassic Period.

Good scientific theories are based on evidence. Did an asteroid collide with the Earth at Nova Scotia at the end of the Triassic Period and cause weather changes that killed many kinds of plants and animals? So far, the evidence for such an event at the Bay of Fundy fossil site is slight.

Elsewhere in the world, though, scientists have found a variety of clues and evidence for a major disaster at this time. For example, in Europe they have found 'shocked quartz', a type of rock usually formed by enormous impacts, such as an asteroid striking the Earth. In Europe, Africa and America, fossils of ancient sea creatures show that almost ninety percent of species alive in Triassic times had disappeared by the Early Jurassic Period.

Just as the pieces of a jigsaw puzzle interlock to make a single image, so geological information from various fossil sites has combined to reveal the geological changes in Nova Scotia at the end of the Triassic.

A NEW WORLD
MANA PARK
GAME RESERVE
Zimbabwe
200 million years ago

In a world that is largely dry, herds of large plant-eaters browse on vegetation beside streams and shallow ponds. Packs of predators patrol these lowland waterways, looking for prey to hunt and corpses to scavenge.

WATERSIDE FORESTS

The landscape of what is now southern Africa was dry and desert-like 200 million years ago. Bare sand dunes covered many areas. Yet a wide range of plants, from small ferns to large conifer trees, survived in this harsh environment. Animal life included sturdy fish and primitive mammals. But the rulers of this new period were dinosaurs of many sizes and forms.

The dinosaurs are divided into two groups – bird-hipped and lizard-hipped (see pages 7 and 45). All of the bird-hipped dinosaurs were plant-eaters. The lizard-hipped dinosaurs included all of the meat-eaters and still more plant-eaters.

Scientists say birds evolved from dinosaurs. It seems to make sense that these modern animals would have come from bird-hipped dinosaurs. But two clues suggest that birds grew out of a family of lizard-hipped meat-eaters. The first piece of evidence comes from the earliest bird, *Archaeopteryx*, which had lizard hips. The second clue comes from the most bird-like dinosaurs, which were small lizard-hipped carnivores.

The mammals of ancient Zimbabwe were shrew-like in size. Scientists think that some of their habits and body features were also shrew-like. They spent a long time on the ground.

A ***Massospondylus* walks** beneath spreading araucarian conifers. These trees grew worldwide in the early Jurassic and still survive in the Southern Hemisphere. We call them monkey puzzle trees. A tiny *Megazostrodon* mammal high in a tree snatches a beetle in its sharp front teeth. Scientists think *Megazostrodon* might have moved up and down among the trees.

Mana Park Game Reserve – Today
Palaeontologist Mike Raath walks with his camera beside the fossil site in Mana Park Game Reserve. The soft sandstone banks of the Zambezi River hold fossils, including those of dinosaurs, from 200 million years ago.

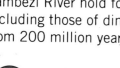

Fossils from Early Jurassic Mana Park show that the mammals had one set of milk teeth and then one set of permanent teeth – as we do. (Reptiles keep changing their teeth throughout life.) These shrew-like mammals were probably active at night, or in twilight, when they would be less vulnerable to carnivorous dinosaurs and other predators. The high branches of the araucarian trees would have also provided safety from predators. The tiny mammals probably scrambled up the tree trunks when they felt threatened.

By the Early Jurassic Period, dinosaurs were the largest animals on land. The first mammals had evolved from cynodont reptiles. Plants were slower to change. Many types survived from the Triassic.

ANIMALS
1. *Erythrotherium* (eh-RITH-ro-THEER-ee-um)
2. *Lesothosaurus* (less-OO-too-SAW-rus)
3. *Massospondylus* (MASS-o-SPON-di-lus)
4. *Megazostrodon* (MEG-a-ZOSS-tro-don)
5. *Semionotus* (SEM-ee-o-NO-tus)
6. *Syntarsus* (sin-TAR-sus)

PLANTS
7. Cycads (SY-kads) and araucarian conifers (AR-or-CARE-ee-uns)
8. Cycadeoid (sy-KAD-ee-oyd)

ALSO AT THIS SITE: *Dicroidium* ferns (DIE-crow-ID-ee-um)

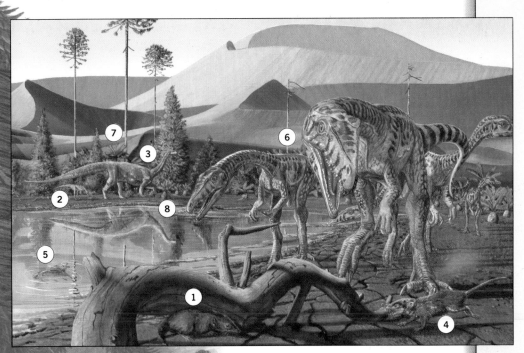

Mana Park Game Reserve – Then

A *Syntarsus* dinosaur pack prowls the shore of a shallow lake. In the background, huge sand dunes stretch into the distance. Where the dinosaurs' feet disturb the ground, the tiny mammals called *Megazostrodon* and *Erythrotherium* scurry underfoot looking for insects to eat. Plant-eating dinosaurs, the little *Lesothosaurus* and the larger *Massospondylus,* nervously watch the predators from a safe distance. *Semionotus* fish swim in the lake. Vegetation crowds the shore, including ferns, squat cycadeoids, taller cycads called *Dicroidium*, and towering araucarian trees.

Zimbabwe, Then and Now

Today, Zimbabwe lies in hot, humid southeastern Africa. In the Early Jurassic, it was hotter and drier as part of the southern continent, Gondwana.

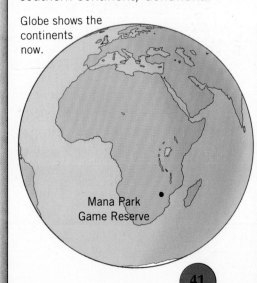

Globe shows the continents now.

Mana Park Game Reserve

DINOSAURS DOMINATE

PLANTS

Because humans belong in the mammal group, even scientists have sometimes thought of mammals as the 'best' animals. But for 135 million years, the dinosaurs formed the more important group. It is doubtful that dinosaurs even noticed the mammals in their world, except as an occasional snack.

MEGAZOSTRODON
Meaning of name: 'Large girdle tooth' – after the girdle, or rim, round the top of each of its teeth.
Order: Triconodonta
Size, Weight: 13 centimetres long, under 225 grams
Location: Lesotho, southern Africa
Diet: Insects and other invertebrates

Megazostrodon belongs to one of the earliest groups of mammals, the triconodonts, named after the three points on each of their back teeth. *Megazostrodon*'s body shape is known from a complete skeleton. It looks like some other early mammals from China and Britain, which somewhat resemble a modern shrew.

MEGAZOSTRODON

The first mammals appeared at the very end of the Triassic Period, but they were different from mammals of today. Most modern mammals bear live young. But scientists think the first mammals laid eggs, like their reptilian ancestors and like such mammals of today as the echidnas and duck-billed platypus.

How can scientists tell that a prehistoric animal was a mammal? They discovered that some extinct animals had teeth, jawbones and ear bones like those of modern mammals. These animals had biting teeth (incisors) in the front, sharp canine teeth for tearing, and premolar and molar teeth for chewing. The lower jaws of these creatures were formed from a single bone, like mammals' jaws. A reptile's lower jaw has several bones. And these animals had a mammal-like combination of three hearing bones. Reptiles have only one.

Beneath majestic conifer trees, cycads and ferns grew in moist areas in the Early Jurassic. Cycads had thick trunks with flat, scaly surfaces like the outsides of pineapples. Fern-like leaves fanned out from their tops. These leaves had holes to let air in and out, unlike the leaves of the closely related cycadeoids.

Ferns came in many forms. Seed ferns had large seeds, trunks like trees and big roots at their bases. These large plants had been growing in wetlands even before there were dinosaurs. Smaller ferns, such as *Dicroidium*, formed a ground cover of vegetation.

Sphenophyllum lay close to the ground and spread into a circle of triangular leaves from a single, central stalk. Grass did not yet exist.

DICROIDIUM

LESOTHOSAURUS
Meaning of name: 'Lizard from Lesotho'
Order: Ornithischia
Size, Weight: 1 metre long, 9 kilos
Location: Southern Africa
Diet: Plants

Lesothosaurus was an early bird-hipped dinosaur. A horn-covered tip on its snout helped *Lesothosaurus* snip plants, which were then chopped up by teeth of varied shapes. Teeth in the sides of its jaw were shaped like arrowheads, perhaps for gripping.

SYNTARSUS

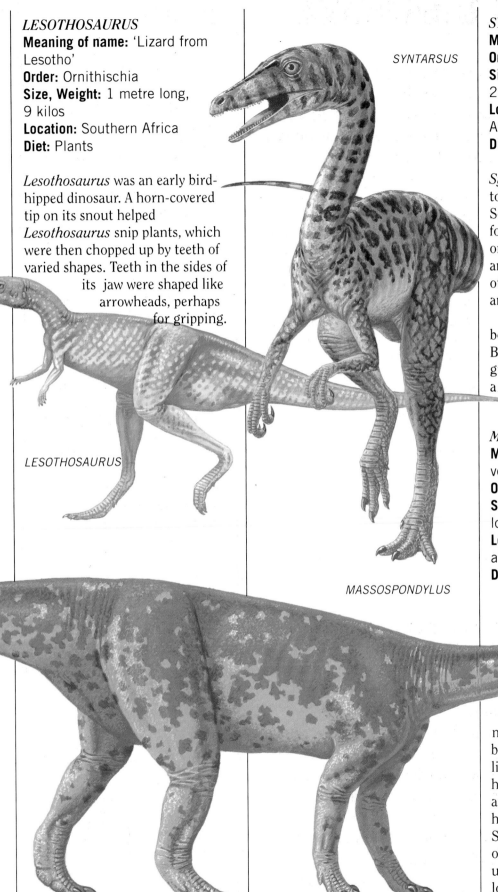

LESOTHOSAURUS

MASSOSPONDYLUS

SYNTARSUS
Meaning of name: 'Fused ankle'
Order: Saurischia
Size, Weight: 3 metres long, 23 kilos
Locations: Southern Africa and Arizona
Diet: Meat

Syntarsus was a meat-eater similar to *Coelophysis* from the American Southwest. In Zimbabwe, two adult forms of this dinosaur were found, one about fifteen percent larger and more heavily built than the other. They may represent males and females of the same species.

Syntarsus was narrow, hollow-boned and long-legged, like a stork. But it had sharp, curved teeth, grasping three-fingered hands and a long bony tail.

MASSOSPONDYLUS
Meaning of name: 'Longer vertebra'
Order: Saurischia
Size, Weight: 3.5 to 5 metres long, 225 kilos
Locations: Zimbabwe and Arizona
Diet: Plants

Massospondylus is a well-known prosauropod. Parts of more than eighty skeletons have been found. *Massospondylus* was lightly built and medium-sized. Its head was small and narrow. Its eyes and nostrils were large, so it may have had keen vision and smell. Some of its teeth had grooves and others were flat. Its upper jaw was unusual, projecting beyond its lower jaw. The lower jaw may have had a beak covering the bone.

43

AFRICAN WATER HOLES

In dry regions of the world, animals gather in lowlands where water is more often found. In the valleys of the Serengeti Plain of East Africa today, the need for water during dry seasons forces animals to visit watering holes. Some visit infrequently. Other kinds have to drink every day. The same thirst drove plant-eating and meat-eating dinosaurs to gather in the valleys of southern Africa during the Early Jurassic Period. Here they could find the lakes and water holes that were vital for life.

Whatever the climate, smaller carnivores may form groups to hunt together. Coordinated pack hunting enables these animals to take down prey much larger than themselves. Lions in modern southern Africa gather where game is plentiful. They combine to pull down zebras and wildebeests, tearing at them until they are too weakened to resist. Usually the females do the hunting; the males live off their kills. Using the same strategy, packs of *Syntarsus* dinosaurs may have killed *Massospondylus*, even though these herbivores were quite large.

A lion and lioness feast on an African buffalo at a water hole in Serengeti National Park in East Africa. Buffalo are fierce, but they are no match for lions working as a team. Predators have evolved greater speeds, higher intelligence and keener senses to give them an advantage in their battles of wits and their struggles with prey.

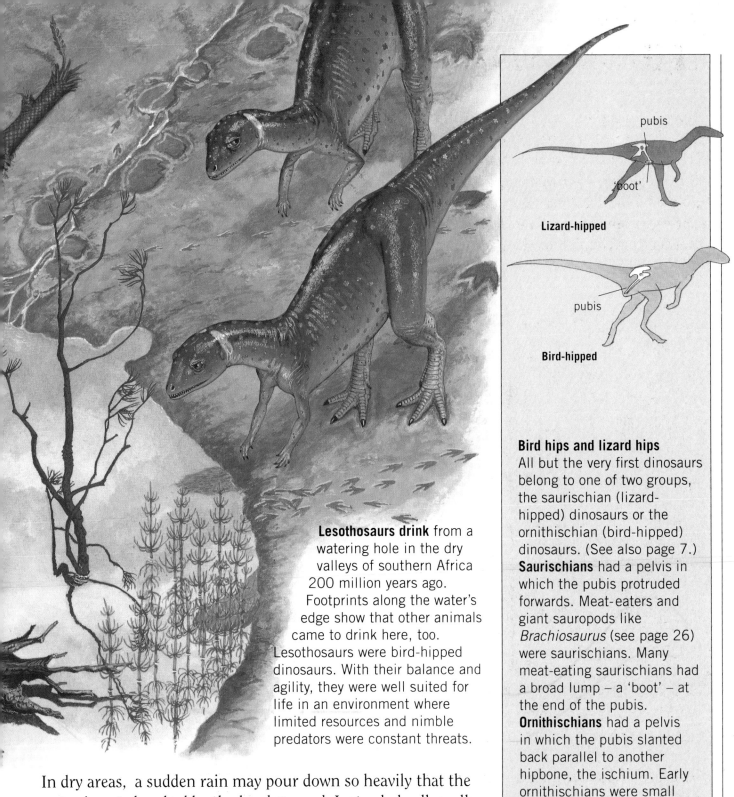

Lesothosaurs drink from a watering hole in the dry valleys of southern Africa 200 million years ago. Footprints along the water's edge show that other animals came to drink here, too. Lesothosaurs were bird-hipped dinosaurs. With their balance and agility, they were well suited for life in an environment where limited resources and nimble predators were constant threats.

pubis

'boot'

Lizard-hipped

pubis

Bird-hipped

Bird hips and lizard hips

All but the very first dinosaurs belong to one of two groups, the saurischian (lizard-hipped) dinosaurs or the ornithischian (bird-hipped) dinosaurs. (See also page 7.)

Saurischians had a pelvis in which the pubis protruded forwards. Meat-eaters and giant sauropods like *Brachiosaurus* (see page 26) were saurischians. Many meat-eating saurischians had a broad lump – a 'boot' – at the end of the pubis.

Ornithischians had a pelvis in which the pubis slanted back parallel to another hipbone, the ischium. Early ornithischians were small two-legged plant-eaters. Later ones included large duckbills and many four-legged plant-eaters. Their hips gave these animals a lower centre of gravity, helping them to hold their balance in spite of their big stomachs.

In dry areas, a sudden rain may pour down so heavily that the water is not absorbed by the hard ground. Instead, deadly walls of water rush down the valleys, threatening wildlife. Entire herds may be wiped out as a flash flood sweeps across them. Such disasters sometimes kill caribou in Canada and wildebeests in the Serengeti Plain of East Africa. In southern Africa 200 million years ago, floods may have overtaken herds of dinosaurs when rivers quickly swelled with rain. Their bodies rotted away and the bones of some of them became fossilized.

MASS DROWNING

In 1972, palaeontologist Dr Michael Raath was walking along an elephant track to a river in the Zambezi Valley when he saw something that, in his words, made his hair stand up. Ahead of him was a treasure trove of dinosaur bones, remains of a catastrophe 200 million years ago. The bones of many *Syntarsus* meat-eaters were exposed there (see page 43). The remains included complete skeletons of both adults and juveniles.

THE KILLER FLOOD

A pack of *Syntarsus*, young and old, walks across a sandy plain (**1**). Sudden torrential rains produce a flash flood from the hills (**2**). In panic, the dinosaurs scatter. They swim well, but the flood is so strong that the entire pack is swept under and drowned (**3**). The flood recedes, leaving decaying bodies covered by sand. Minerals seep into the bones and preserve them in detail for 200 million years.

The fossils were embedded in fine-grained sandstone that showed the dinosaurs had died among sand dunes. Dr Raath concluded that they died suddenly, in a flash flood.

The bones were so well preserved that Dr Raath could see the grooves where blood vessels once ran through them and the places where muscle tendons had been attached. Another South African scientist, Dr Anusuya Chinsamy, studied these fossils under a microscope and added new evidence in many areas of dinosaur research – from how dinosaurs grew, moved and used energy, to how they died and became fossils.

Studies of many specimens of *Syntarsus* and *Massospondylus* have also added new evidence to an on-going debate: Were dinosaurs warm- or cold-blooded? The bones of these species – as in most but not all dinosaurs – have growth rings like those seen in trees. Among animals, growth rings are usually marks of cold-blooded animals like reptiles.

COLD- OR WARM-BLOODED?

Cross sections of the bones of cold-blooded animals show distinct rings of growth. Bone growth is not constant. It slows and speeds up in regular cycles, perhaps by year or season.

1. The bones of the plant-eating dinosaur *Massospondylus* show growth rings (seen here in close-up as lines), like a cold-blooded animal has. But the bones of some dinosaurs show no rings of growth when viewed in cross-section.

2. The bones of warm-blooded animals show no growth rings as in this section of a bird's bone. These animals grow faster than cold-blooded animals do and at a more even speed as they reach adulthood.

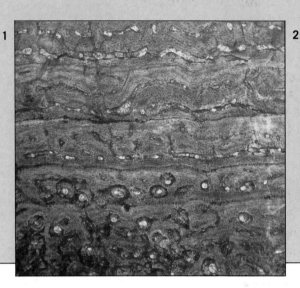
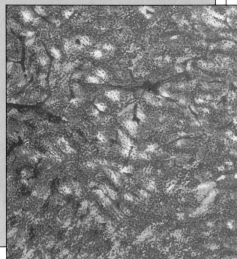

A palaeontologist on Dr Raath's team chisels away at rock in the Zambezi River Valley, looking for more *Syntarsus* fossils. The gentle covering of fine sand kept the bones in position after the animals drowned and their flesh rotted away.

How might a warm-blooded or cold-blooded dinosaur have behaved? Warm-blooded animals like mammals and birds have a built-in control that keeps their body temperatures constant. A warm-blooded dinosaur might have had the endurance to move quickly for long periods of time. But it would have also needed vast amounts of food to fill its energy needs. Cold-blooded animals manage their body temperatures by their activity and by moving between sunlight and shade. A cold-blooded dinosaur would have had much lower energy needs.

Warm-blooded or not, dinosaurs thrived. Some of them evolved into enormous species, and new kinds of dinosaurs replaced other animals, filling many different roles in their environments. From the Early Jurassic until their extinction 65 million years ago, the dinosaurs truly ruled the Earth.

INDEX